THINKING FIT FOR MARRIAGE

THINKING FIT FOR MARRIAGE

Copyright © 2018 Courtney Richards

Published by Beyond Expectations Media

ISBN 978-1-912845-04-0 (sc)

ISBN 978-1-912845-05-7 (e)

All rights reserved. No part of this publication may be reproduced, stored in a retrieval system, or be transmitted, in any form, or by any means, mechanical, electronic, photocopying or otherwise without prior written consent of the publisher.

Any people depicted in stock imagery provided by iStockphoto and Unsplash, are models and such images are being used for illustrative purposes only.

All Scripture quotations marked (NKJV) are from the New King James Version of the Bible. Copyright © 1979, 1980, 1982 by Thomas Nelson, Inc. Used by permission. All rights reserved.

All Scripture quotations marked (AMP) are from the Amplified Bible. Old Testament copyright © 1965, 1987 by Zondervan Corporation. The Amplified New Testament copyright © 1954, 1958, 1987 by the Lockman Foundation. Used by permission. All rights reserved.

All Scripture quotations marked (ESV) are from The Holy Bible, English Standard Version. Copyright © 2001 by Crossways Bibles. Used by permission. All rights reserved.

All Scripture quotations marked (NLT) are from the Holy Bible, New Living Translation. Copyright © 1996, 2004. Used by permission of Tyndale House Publishers. All rights reserved.

All Scripture quotations marked (EXB) are from The Expanded Bible, Copyright © 2011 Thomas Nelson Inc. All rights reserved.

Welcome!

Thank you for taking this journey today. I pray your investment of time is richly rewarded as you open your mind to wisdom and revelation truth about your relationships.

This program can eliminate years pain, disappointment and wasted experiences.

Life is always teaching us something. The lessons we learn from the situations of life are entirely based on our individual worldview. Do you live in a friendly or hostile universe? Einstein said the answer to this question is the most important decision you'll ever make.

3 Great Laws

- The Law of Entropy
- The Law of Observation
- The Law of the Seed

These 3 laws when combined together create something quite spectacular.

The Law of Entropy creates the understanding that we've been given delegated dominion & authority (Genesis 1:28) and unless we do something positive, nature (default position of chaos & disorder) will take its course. We have to enforce order. According to Psalm 1:1 (AMP), we are blessed when we choose not to be a passive and inactive bystander in the situations of life.

The way in which we see & perceive things (The Law of Observation) determines our emotions, our expectations and what we ultimately do about situations and circumstances around us; and The Law of the Seed teaches us that we have the ability and power to change our future by what we do with the seed in our possession today. We have the ability to root out bad seeds and plant new ones for a desired harvest.

Understanding and making use of this knowledge with fundamentally transform your relationships.

Ready, Steady, **SHIFT**

Please circle the Y = yes or the N = no, in answer to the following questions.

Ready

There is time in my life to invest in my own development	Y or N
A gap exists between where I want to be and where I am right now	Y or N
I can work on tasks that will help me to develop and grow	Y or N

Willing

I am willing to perform whatever is necessary to reach my goal and aims	Y or N
I am willing to SHIFT in my thinking concerning relationships and marriage	Y or N
I am willing to attempt new ways of achieving my goals	Y or N

Able

I have the commitment I need to succeed	Y or N
I have the support I need to make significant changes to my life	Y or N
I am mentally ready for a different approach to my life	Y or N
I am physically prepared for the encounters I may not have experienced before	Y or N

7-10 Y This program will be effective, exciting and rewarding for you

5-7 Y You may need to make some adjustments before starting this program

1-5 Y You are not interested in SHIFTING!

What do you want to get from this program?..
....

THINKING FIT FOR MARRIAGE

Use the notes sections in this workbook to make notes whilst the facilitator takes you through the session.

Did you know that there are around 250,000 marriages in Britain each year costing around £2.5Bn

No-one gets married expecting to get divorced (unless it's a business arrangement). However, at a ratio of nearly 1 in 2 and costing around £40,000 per couple, there are around 115,000 divorces every year.

OUR AIM
Relating—and the quality of our relationships—is of deep, natural, and inherent concern for all of us and like any human endeavour, takes attention, care, and commitment. This program is designed to help you create a SHIFT in your thinking that supports the building of strong relationships allowing you to flourish whether single or married.
For those that are already married, it could serve as a means of identifying where things may have gone wrong and a platform for making things better.

You'll discover a possibility of being related independent of your past, your expectations, your preferences, or your views—a dimension more powerful than personality or circumstance—a dimension where relationships can become an occasion for creativity, vitality, intimacy, and self-expression.

Marriage Beyond Expectations:

- We offer specialist programs covering various aspects of improving relationships.
- We also offer Mediation/ Conflict Resolution service & Relationship Coaching
- Get in touch on 07957125137 or
  hello@marriagebeyondexpectations.com
  www.marriagebeyondexpectations.com

Do not be conformed to this world, but be transformed by the renewal of your mind, that by testing you may discern what is the will of God, what is good and acceptable and perfect. Romans 12:2 ESV

Our quest is to wage war on diseased thinking and to embed the divine truth.

The Purpose of Relationships - Generally

And He has made from **one blood** every nation of men to dwell on all the face of the earth, and has determined their pre-appointed times and the boundaries of their dwellings, (Acts 17:26 NKJV)

1.1 Relationship - describes the type and condition of your connection to another person.

1.2 Without knowing how to relate to another human being effectively – we stand no hope of succeeding in marriage.

1.3 Like it or not, one of the most fundamental facts of our existence is that we are all connected (related). However, without knowing the purpose of a connection abuse will always happen.

1.4 You don't have to be friends to be connected. For example, David and Goliath were in a relationship. The Children of Israel and Pharaoh were also in a relationship.
David's actions showed that he had revelation when he said "isn't there a cause" to his brother who was questioning his reason for being at the battlefield.

1.5 Sometimes our connection could be to bring healing, other times it may be to bring reproof, other times it may be for multiplication of your efforts.

1.6 In an employment situation, we are in a relationship - the terms of which are outlined in a contract of employment. This states the terms, conditions and expectations of the connection - the chief purpose being to bring increase to the organisation

1.7 In the case of marriage, a union unlike any other, and against the backdrop of challenges, joys and pain - each person gets the opportunity to practice Godly qualities like patience, love and forgiveness.

1.8 God is good and has a purpose for our lives. Therefore, **we need to:**

- Know by divine revelation our own global purpose.
- Know by revelation the purpose and outcome of our connection to another human or If the purpose of the connection is unknown, to know that it is God's will.
- Strategies in how to get the most out of this relationship (fulfilling God's will) - by (a) understanding diversity, (b) taking actions led by the Holy Spirit that are love actions - independent and not based on pre-qualifying the recipient's worthiness to receive.

IMPORTANT NOTE
Without understanding human relationships in general, we have no hope of making a success of marriage.

The Origins
God placed an inherent command into all living things to increase Genesis 1:22, and this increase comes through relationships - our interconnectedness to others.

- The first relationship the bible speaks of is the one Adam had with God the father. Created at the end of Day six, he learns to rest in God.
- From this he learns his identity (self-image), purpose and work Gen 1:22 & 26, 2:15-20a, 23-24
- Next, he receives specific instructions from God Gen 2:16-17
- The second relationship we learn about is Eve's arrival and her first relationship was with God (Adam was asleep) Gen 2:21-22
- The third relationship we learn about is Adam's relationship with his wife Eve and their joint relationship with God. Gen 2:18, 23-25
- The fourth relationship we find is Eve's relationship with the serpent and the consequences of them both believing false information Gen 3

EXPOSING & EXPLODING DISEASED THINKING ABOUT MARRIAGE

2. Marriage is important & great, but so is being single... We need to stop our lopsided worship of marriage.
It is important to see marriage in the right context and therefore important to dispel the many myths, sayings and half-truths surrounding this institution.

2.1 Wedded bliss
This saying assumes that marriage has no problems, when the scriptures say the opposite **1 Cor. 7:28 EXB** *But if you do marry, you have not sinned [in doing so]; and if a virgin marries, she has not sinned [in doing so]. Yet those [who marry] will have troubles (special challenges) in this life, and I am trying to spare you that.*

2.2 Soul mate
This forms part of popular culture that says we have another human being that was created just for us. It originates from Greek mythology and is not part of God's order.

2.3 The other half
Assumes you're not whole by yourself

2.4 My better half
Assumes you're not whole by yourself and a position of false humility / self-abasement – you are fearfully and wonderfully made. see **Ps 139:16-17**

2.5 Marriage will complete me
Wrong! You are expecting something from marriage it wasn't designed to fulfil. You are complete in him **(Col. 2:10)**. If another person could do it, a relationship with God would be irrelevant. God will never give you a gift that will replace his presence. That is why your mate is not designed to

produce your joy. The presence of God creates joy. "In your presence is fullness of joy" **(Psalm 16:11)** - Fullness implies "requiring nothing in addition."

2.6 **The odd one out**
Compared to those that are married this assumes there's a problem with being single.

2.7 **Fairy Tales**
Tell of Prince Charming coming to rescue the princess. Hollywood – Happily ever after... We have been bombarded with unrealistic images of marriage.

2.8 Fantasy thinking - Through our lopsided importance of romance, we have created erotic fantasies that place us in an altered state of reality and creates a demand that is unable to be fulfilled or sustained by anyone. This leads to unhappiness and the disappointment of un-realised expectations.

2.9 Many men marry women hoping they'll never change. **Many women** marry men hoping to change them. Both these viewpoints ultimately lead to unhappiness and the disappointment of un-realised expectations.

2.10 Some people believe that marrying a gifted person will guarantee it will work... You are marrying the person's character, **NOT** their anointing!

2.11 **The Lord told me to marry her/ him. I saw her/him in a dream....**
I'm not questioning your revelation. However, there is no scriptural basis showing God appointing spouses to anyone – Hosea was told to marry a prostitute but not which one. Joseph had already chosen to take Mary as his wife when the angel spoke to him.

This way of conducting our lives leads to us abdicating responsibility for our decisions – blaming the God, the devil or each other for what was ultimately our choice.
Genesis 1:26 & Duet 30:19 says that God delegates to us choice – let them rule...

Matthew 19:6 What God put together let no man put asunder...
We choose by looking with expectation to find... However, God in giving his blessing to our choice puts us together.

He who finds a wife finds a good thing - this infers searching, finding, being found & choosing – God doesn't drop it into your lap. He does however, provide guidance for those seeking.
i.e. You meet someone and God says "step away!" or you meet someone and God says "he/ she's fine"

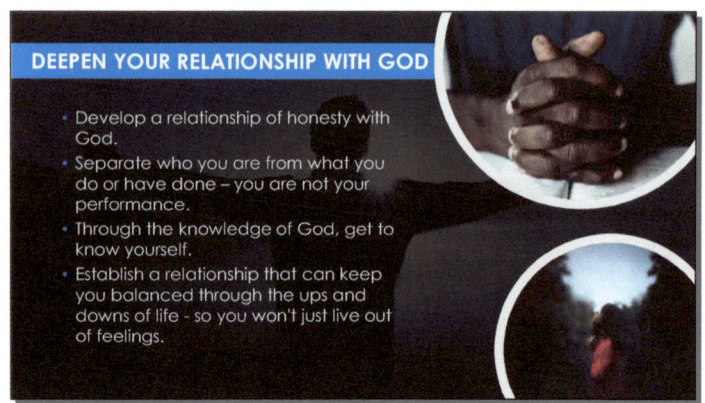

The true essence of marriage is a dimension where your relationship can become an occasion for creativity, vitality, intimacy and self-expression. **3.** Deep within the heart of every human, is the desire to be loved and accepted - doing almost anything to achieve it.

3.1 Develop a relationship of honesty with God. Allow God into every room of your heart. **Psalm 51:6**

3.2 Separate who you are from what you do or have done - you are not your performance. We often see God and our relationships in a performance related lens. **Ephesians 1:6 & 2:8-9. Luke 10:38-42. Romans 5:8**

3.3 Through the knowledge of God, we get to know ourselves. **Matthew 16:17**

3.4 The fact that relationships fluctuate in their intensity and enjoyment - we need to establish a relationship that doesn't change - that can keep us balanced through the ups and downs of life - so we won't just live out of our feelings. Your faith and belief systems need to stay balanced. This helps us to not be spiritually bipolar - swinging from pole to pole of emotions. **Romans 8:38-39**

3.5 A single person's relationship with God has the potential to be deeper than he/she who is married - purely on a practical level, your focus will be divided between caring about pleasing your spouse and pleasing God. **1 Cor. 7:32-34**

Are you SHIFTING?

For example, I thought……. (old beliefs, I now reject), today I'm moving towards (new beliefs)…

List the ways below:

SEEK A WHOLE LIFE AS A SINGLE PERSON

- Stop treating being single like it's some kind of disease.
- When God created everything - he said it was good - including you.
- You are complete in him. You don't need marriage to make you whole. You are already whole.

4. In Genesis 3, Adam and Eve were trying to attain something that they already had and as a consequence, lost their power, authority & rule. When you chase marriage to give you significance, you lose your power to achieve all that God placed in you.

4.1 Stop treating being single like it's some kind of disease
4.2 When God created everything - he said it was good - including you.
4.3 You are complete in him. You don't need marriage to make you whole. You are already whole. **Matt 19:10-12. Psalm 139:16-17**

- ✓ You are not defined by what you do - job
- ✓ You are not defined by your physical form - looks/ appearance
- ✓ You are not defined by your possessions - stuff
- ✓ You are not defined by your past - yesterday
- ✓ You are not defined by your marital status - marriage

What can you do to get your power back?

List what you'll need to **start, stop or continue**.

JUNK IN THE TRUNK

The various personal issues we bring to a marriage... if not dealt with will cause a number of problems.

5. There are various personal issues and thinking errors we bring to a marriage that if not corrected will cause a number of problems.

The list below isn't exhaustive, but points to many common issues. Choose to make the necessary changes and if necessary, seek help from a suitable professional or pastoral advisor.

1. **Angry outbursts** – anger is energy requiring a focus. *"Be angry but sin not..."* Behind anger is most frequently, some form of fear. You may believe that you have a right to visit your behaviour on others - **Let it go!** *"They made me angry..."* No, anger was already in you – the situation just brought out that what was already in you. **Let it go!**

2. **Abusive behaviours** – Without knowing the use of a thing, abuse is inevitable. Abuse comes in a variety of forms - ranging from emotional to physical – but is ultimately wrong use.

3. **Intimidation** – You get your own way by shouting at others, putting them down, threatening others. Your behaviours at trying to control others is a form of witchcraft – **Stop it. Stop it now!**

4. **Vindictive** – You punish others for making choices you didn't agree with. A form of un-Godly control.

5. **Silence when you are upset** – this is a form of control / manipulation

6. **Co-dependency** - You've surrendered correct order and placed another human at the centre of your life (instead of God). Now your behaviours and emotions are tied and controlled by what's happening to another person.

7. **Jealousy** - This is an emotional cancer that eats you up from the inside. By not being content with what you have or where you are - you desire that which belongs to another. This ultimately steals your peace and joy and causes issues in the relationships you have.

8. **Previous sexual relationships, bringing the past relationship into the present**. Stop poisoning your future with your past. Look forward – stop looking back.

9. **Old emotional hurts** i.e. rejection - **Let it go!** Release the fears

10. **Trust issues** – Trust is built on capability, commitment & consistency. We have to develop trust – but this needs to be qualified. Did you previously trust someone that didn't display these needed qualities? You need to evaluate the people around you. Just because someone failed you doesn't mean everyone else will – **Let it go**.
    Now, on the other side, do you trust yourself? Don't project your own trust issues on others.

11. **Lack of commitment** – You have a mortgage, a car loan but say you're afraid to commit - **sort it out!** Seek help to look at the real reasons.
    If you are with someone that demonstrates lack of commitment – walk on by...

12. **Integrity** – Do you do what you say you'll do? Make a decision to embed this character trait.

13. **Selfishness** – The opposite of love isn't hate – it's selfishness. If you want to continue being selfish – you aren't ready for marriage. With selfishness comes mean & stinginess. At the centre of marriage is love - the desire to give to another at the expense of yourself (selflessness).

14. **Responsibility** – Do you take responsibility for your life? Do you expect someone else to pick up the tab?
    Enshrined in our humanity is the power of choice. Responsibility cannot be separated from choice. Embrace the divine command to manage your own life. Genesis 1:26-28

15. **Decisions made out of fear** - Settling for the wrong person for fear of being left on the shelf.

16. Generalised stinking thinking like all men are dogs, liars & thieves etc.

What changes are you going to commit to making? List them.

For further insights and information on thinking errors, get a copy of
I Am What You Say I Am Courtney Richards

6. "It seemed like a good idea at the time…"
There are many overt and covert reasons underpinning the need to get married. Therefore, making a lifelong commitment without due diligence or attention to what you are undertaking is a sure recipe for later problems. Marriage is easy and relatively inexpensive to do, but unravelling a poor decision is both emotionally, spiritually and financially draining.

Below are some dodgy reasons for getting married.
The list below isn't exhaustive, but points to many common issues.
Choose to make the necessary changes and if necessary, seek help from a suitable professional or pastoral advisor.

1. Tick-tock, biological clock!
2. You found your dream dress.
3. To have sex.
4. If you've had sex and are trying to avoid feeling condemned.
5. For my lust issue to go away.
6. To cure loneliness.
7. Thinking he'll change, or I'll be able to change him… *Don't kid yourself – you're not that powerful.*
8. You think you can't live without him/ her. (In him we live, move and have our being)
9. Financial security…
10. Marriage will fix what is broken in your relationship.
11. You want to tick marriage off your to-do list.
12. Your parents, friends or the church are pressuring you.
13. Because he asked.
14. To have a fairy-tale wedding.
15. You are having his baby.
16. You can't bear being <u>single</u> any longer.
17. You are crazy in love and have never been in one fight!
18. All my friends have or are getting married.

DEVELOP INTERESTS BEYOND WORK, HOME & CHURCH

- Widen your field of interest
- Interest makes you interesting and adds flavour to relationships.
- Learn to enjoy your own company

7. Life is more than just home, work & church!

We serve a God of all creation - full of diversity and invention. We need to stop living such insular and one-dimensional lives. We are further encouraged to go into all the world... meaning go into all facets of human existence and bring the light of God's Kingdom.

7.1 Widen your field of interest – be it arts, science, bird watching, technology – you choose!

7.2 Interest makes you interesting and adds flavour to relationships.

7.3 After the euphoria of sex has worn off, what do you have in common?

7.4 What are your interests? Otherwise life will be dry and boring, and you'll find yourself falling out of love.

7.5 Read books to expand your mind. Grow your interests..

NOTE: If you don't like your own company, why should anyone else...?

What interest(s) can you start to develop in the next 30 days? List them

Beloved, I pray that in every way you may succeed and prosper and be in good health physically, just as I know your soul prospers spiritually 3 John 1:2 AMP

8. Exercise your body and mind - It is important to view yourself holistically as spirit, soul and body. They all need exercise and development to achieve and sustain your highest potential.

8.1 Renewal of the mind is essential to fulfil the divine plan for your life **(Rom 12:2)** & while bodily exercise is of some value **1 Tim 4:8**
This doesn't mean don't exercise but that great physical fitness comes from a great mind.

Giving the following benefits:
8.2 Better for mind and bodily health.

8.3 Reduces stress and increases resilience

8.4 Longevity & enjoyment of life

8.5 Overcoming personal fitness battles strengthens the mind and body & teaches mastery over your body – bringing it into subjection.

> **What will you commit to doing to increase your mental and physical fitness?**

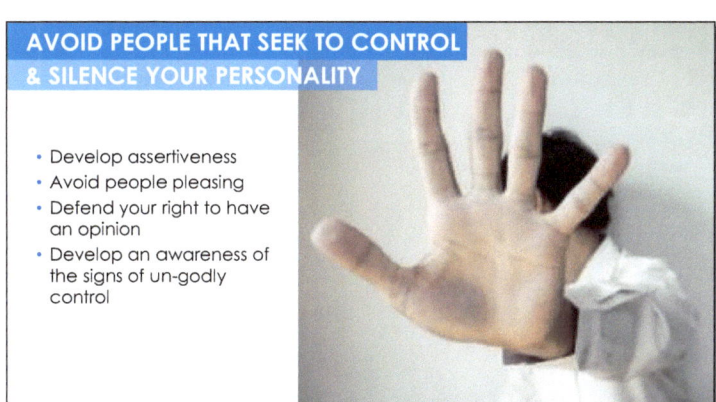

9. Avoid people that seek to control & silence your personality - irrespective of their sex. Keep away from manipulative people...

9.1 Assertiveness – knowing what you believe for yourself & knowing what to do – taking independent action, and not being swayed by others. *Who hindered you from knowing the truth?*

9.2 Its alright for someone not to agree with you & vice versa. We are entitled to a different point of view.

9.3 Run from people that:
- ✓ get angry
- ✓ put on the waterworks
- ✓ threaten you
- ✓ punish you
- ✓ put you down in the face of different opinions

9.4 People Pleasing – Not putting the pleasing of man above the pleasing of God – peer pressure. *What can man do to me?* **Hebrews 13:6**

9.5 Avoid people that have behaviours of ungodly control....
- ✓ Know what you actually believe
- ✓ Be not afraid of man
- ✓ Know that we have dominion over everything God made - with one exception - each other (Genesis 1:26-28). Trying to dominate another human for your own benefit is a form of witchcraft.

What will you **start, stop or continue** to see better results?

SET A GUARD ON YOUR HEART
- Don't allow your heart to get carried away with every compliment
- Don't allow yourself to be intoxicated with anything
- It's easier to guard your heart when you value yourself.
- Know what's not safe for your heart.

Guard your heart above all else, for it determines the course of your life.
Proverbs 4:23 NLT

10. Set a guard on your heart
Of preeminent importance, we are to guard the entry points to our heart... We all have different '*soft spots*' and it's responsibility to know ourselves and guard our heart.

- ✓ Don't allow your heart to get carried away with every compliment
- ✓ Beware of developing soul ties.
- ✓ Beware of having intimate conversations out of their place...
- ✓ Beware of wanting something that isn't there. Expecting someone to desire you, when they're clearly not that into you!
- ✓ Don't allow yourself to be intoxicated with anything mankind does.
- ✓ It's easier to guard your heart when you value yourself - create boundaries & maintain for your life
- ✓ Know what's not safe for your heart.

10.1 Avoid opening up yourself to the wrong person? Women of Jerusalem, promise me by the gazelles and the deer of the field not to awaken or excite (arouse) love until it is ready (a warning to the women to wait for love until the right person comes along) Songs of Solomon 2:7 EXB

10.2 Respect marriage - If you feel you're getting too familiar with someone that's married - don't be a spare tyre. Don't cross certain lines. Respect marriage, but don't worship it.

NOTES

Are you SHIFTING?

For example, I thought……. (old beliefs, I now reject), today I'm moving towards (new beliefs)…

List the ways below:

11. Many people when they consider the word lust immediately think of sex. However, lust doesn't just relate to sex, but an overwhelming strong desire for anything, be it sex or cake...
James 1, tells us that we are *"drawn away by our own lust and enticed..."* It is therefore important to know and manage yourself in the light of truth.

11.1 Managing sexual appetite is an acquired behaviour
We all have different appetites – some people love to eat a lot, some little etc...

11.2 Maintaining sexual control will be more of a struggle for some than others - especially if you've had previous sexual relations.

If your appetite is big, this will need to be managed and just like any other craving, it takes effort - its work!

11.3 Know thyself....
- ✓ What is the intensity of your appetite for sex?
- ✓ Develop strategies to manage yourself – self-control is a fruit of the spirit.
- ✓ Know your own triggers.
- ✓ **Saying you can't help it isn't acceptable!**

> What actions will you **start, stop or continue** to bring order to this aspect of your life? List the ways below.

KEEP IT SIMPLE

- Avoid decisions that make your life more complicated
- Live and budget within your means
- Having sex before marriage will impair your objectivity and ultimately your decision making capacity

12. Try not to make decisions that complicate your life - Having babies as a single parent is achievable but is an added complication to life. Keep things simple.

12.1 Having sex before marriage will impair your objectivity and ultimately your decision-making capacity. It also sets the wrong foundation for the future relationship.
It is like hiring a builder and paying them before the job is done!

12.2 Live and budget within your means - when you live outside your means it affects your life - **period!** You're then not looking for a messiah to get you out of trouble...

> What actions will you **start, stop or continue** to simplify your life?
>
> List the ways below.

13. Confirmation Bias

Dopamine is a neuro-transmitter in the brain that generates feelings of pleasure. You get a shot of this *'feel-good juice'* when you're right about something. In human interactions, we tend to latch onto initial feelings and then look for evidence to confirm what we already think (confirmation bias) - getting a shot of dopamine for every time we're proved right – even if it's to our own long-term detriment.

In relationships this can be disastrous, as our pre-conceived bias can cause you to make poor decisions.
For example, you meet the man/ woman of your dreams and he's / she's the one you've been waiting for etc... Everything he or she does and what you perceive serves only to confirm what you already believe... often missing RED FLAGS of trouble.

It is therefore important to get to know yourself and your true feelings. Psalm 51 talks about having *"truth on the inward parts."* Ask the Holy Spirit to help you to know the real truth.
Romans 12:2 encourages you to "renew your mind *that by testing you may discern what is the will of God, what is good and acceptable and perfect."*

RED FLAGS!

13.1 RED FLAG! If you don't possess a passionate desire to give to them.
The proof of love is the desire to give. **John 3:16**. Too often marriage becomes an exchange. Exchange is the evidence of business, not love. At the most basic level, love is so much more than an emotion – it is the decision to give. To give at the expense of yourself to someone else without expecting anything in return.

13.2 RED FLAG! If they don't possess a passionate desire to give back to you.
Not necessarily expensive gifts, or huge amounts of money. A listening ear, flexibility and patience are gifts.

13.3 RED FLAG! It they ignore the counsel of qualified mentors in their life. This rebellion against sound wisdom shows they are living an un-disciplined and un-advised life.

13.4 RED FLAG! If they have an obsession to attract the attention of the opposite sex.

13.5 RED FLAG! If breaking the law is humorous and exciting to them.

13.6 RED FLAG! If it's obvious that their focus is elsewhere.

13.7 RED FLAG! If they refuse to find a job!

13.8 RED FLAG! If there exists regular strife between them and their parents.

13.9 RED FLAG! If you cannot trust them in your absence

13.10 Caution! If the feedback from you or others releases a flood of anger.

13.11 Caution! If they continuously give you counsel contrary to the word of God.

13.12 Caution! If they are uncomfortable in the presence of God.

Extra's to consider. Are they:
- Selfish?
- Vindictive?
- Stingy?
- A thief?
- A gambler?
- Violent?
- Manipulative?
- Discouraging?
- Excited by worldly stuff?

PAY ATTENTION!
- People show you facets of themselves every day.
- How do they act/ react under pressure?
- What character traits are frequently on display?
- Be aware of things that affect your judgement.
- Be mindful of your own bias

14. **ACTIVITY**: Listening Exercise

- **Did you get some wrong?** Most people are likely to have made mistakes
- **What caused you to get some wrong?** The biggest cause is assumptions. Usually made from limited information being provided and on your previous experiences, (You may have heard this story or a similar one before) causing you to 'fill in the blanks' of missing information yourself.

While this was a humorous quiz– it throws up an important question.
What are the consequences of not listening/ paying attention in our relationships?

People reveal themselves every day – pay attention:
- ✓ To how do they act/ react under pressure?
- ✓ What character traits are frequently on display?

14.1 Adam observed the characteristics of each animal before naming them. He did the same when he saw Eve, before saying she was compatible for him and choosing her as his wife.

- ✓ **Pay attention to people.**
- ✓ **Looking at how they act & how they react... Make your decisions based on observable behaviours.**

14.2 As human beings, given all the listening we do, you'd think we'd be good at it. In fact, this often not the case due to the amount of information we are continually presented with.

Remember and apply these keys when listening to people.

- Using listening skills involves more than just hearing the words that are spoken.

- Aim to also pay attention to the feelings and emotions that are being expressed and the intention and commitment the individual is showing to the issue at hand.

14.3 Did your familiarity with the story hinder your ability to pay full attention?

For example, based on past experience, you may think you know what a person is going to say or do or the intention of their heart only to be completely wrong.

The term hidden in plain sight refers to our inability to distinguish or perceive information in front of us because our attention is being drawn to something else.

Be careful of your own lusts (passionate desires) – Eve was drawn away and enticed because of her own lust. She ended up confusing the issue and making a disastrous decision.

> What actions will you **start, stop or continue** to better your ability to pay attention?
>
> List the ways below.

Caution! Before you say "*I do...*"

15. The universal warning sign alerts us to potential danger. When driving a car if you see a warning sign ignite on the instrument panel, you won't need to make an immediate stop, but advises you to check it out at your earliest opportunity. Choosing to ignore the warning sign is costly, as later you'll see a red warning sign which means a large repair bill.

When choosing a mate pay attention to all warning signs, then thoroughly investigate before proceeding further.

- ✓ The list below isn't exhaustive, but points to many common warning signs.
- ✓ Choose to make the necessary changes and if necessary, seek help from a suitable professional or pastoral advisor.

15.1 Caution! If your personal achievements do not create excitement in them.
Pay attention to those you love to celebrate with. True love does get upset with the success of another, but instead joins in the celebration.

15.2 Caution! If they never ask quality questions concerning your greatest dreams and goals. The desire to learn more about you through deep questions is an important quality for a mate.

15.3 Caution! If you don't see continuous improvement in the relationship. Improvement points to growth, so the relationship will be either green and growing or ripe and rotting.

15.4 Caution! If they show little regard for timekeeping or the schedule of others.

15.5 Caution! If they have not exited a previous relationship peacefully. Some people love drama.

15.6 Caution! If their parents have contempt for you or your purpose in life.

15.7 Caution! If they frequently make a mountain out of a molehill issue.

15.8 Caution! If they feel inferior to you.

15.9 Caution! If their own dreams aren't big enough to motivate them.

15.10 Caution! If they regularly treat kindness with ingratitude.

15.11 Caution! If you are not excited about introducing them to those you love.

15.12 Caution! If you cannot trust them with the knowledge of your greatest weakness.

15.13 Caution! If you cannot trust them with your most painful memories.

15.14 Caution! If you cannot trust them with your greatest fears or secrets.

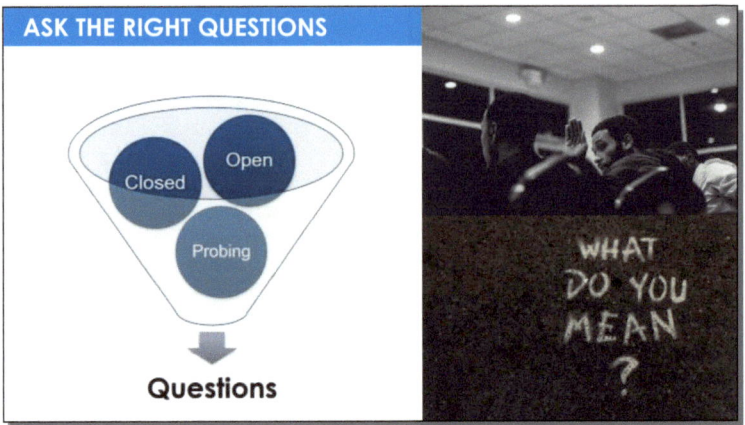

16. Questions help you to learn about others. Don't be afraid of asking thought provoking questions relating to beliefs, values, preferences and goals. You don't want to learn these things after making a lifelong commitment.

Open questions are conversational (can't be answered with a simple yes or no), they enable you to learn about a person. For example, *"what are you views on…?"*

Closed questions are good for confirming details - for example, "Are you coming this evening?"

Probing questions are more searching to truly get to the heart of the matter. For example, *"I noticed you say this but do that, could you explain?"*

For example, one couple had a significant problem after being married because the wife discovered that her husband had always wanted to leave the country and live overseas - expecting her to come with him. Or another one wanted children, but the other didn't.

By asking questions, you'll establish understanding in the following areas:
- ✓ Financial
- ✓ Children (and the approach to bringing them up)
- ✓ Country of residence
- ✓ Dreams and aspirations
- ✓ Important aspects of their past

Below are further questions

16.1 Have they fully surrendered their life to Christ?
Evaluate their attitude to change and transformation. The essence of life with Christ is all about change and this attitude will shape their life.

16.2 Do they get along with others? If they have a history of broken relationships and continual drama, don't expect marriage to be any different. They'll need to get control of their anger, jealousy, pouting sessions and pity parties now, and not after you commit to live the rest of your life with them.

16.3 Do you trust your partner's past? Don't rush into a marriage if you feel unsure about your partner's history—especially if he or she has been married before. It's OK to ask lots of questions. Get all the cards on the table. You don't want to wake up after the honeymoon and learn that your Dr. Jekyll has become a Mr. Hyde.

16.4 How does your family and your partner's family feel about this marriage? There's no guarantee that all parents will be happy with your choices. But if there are major conflicts in the extended family, you may need to assess whether this is a wise decision. Seek pastoral support if family members are trying to stir up conflict. (perhaps they've spotted a **RED FLAG!**)

16.5 Do you and your partner have similar goals and dreams? You don't have to like the same movies or prefer the same kinds of foods. But when God puts two people together, they support each other's dreams. This is especially true when it comes to expectations about children. If your spouse doesn't want kids, and you do, don't assume this will just "work out." If you are a woman who wants a career and your fiancée prefers you to stay home, it's time to re-evaluate.

16.6 Do you and your partner pray together? This is a perfect way to tell if you are spiritually compatible with your partner. If you feel a deep level of spiritual intimacy when you pray with your fiancée, that's a good sign God is putting you together. But if your partner isn't interested in growing spiritually with you, take that as a hint to look elsewhere. When God brings a man and woman together, they should become one in every way.

16.7 Are you financially responsible? You don't have to have boatloads of money to be a happy couple. But if you have not planned how to pay your bills, financial stress will choke your marriage. Be wise. Many couples today have not even learned how to manage a bank account, create a budget or save money. Find a mentor if your parents didn't teach you the basics of money management.

NOTES

> **KEY MESSAGES**
>
> - Marriage isn't a panacea for all the issues in life - marriage, while great is challenging.
> - Get rid of your junk in the trunk - dealing with your personal issues before the "I do's" will save you a lot of headache.
> - Celebrate being single – there's a lot that God can do through you – you're in good company – Jesus!
> - Pay attention!

- ✓ Marriage isn't a panacea for all your issues of life - marriage, while great is challenging.

- ✓ The true essence of marriage is a dimension where your relationship can become an occasion for creativity, vitality, intimacy and self-expression.

- ✓ Marriage is a great place to practice selflessness and the other fruits of the spirit.

- ✓ Get rid of your junk in the trunk - dealing with your personal issues before the "I do's" will save you a lot of headache.

- ✓ Celebrate being single - there's a lot that God can do through you – you're in good company – Jesus was single!

- ✓ Pay attention!

> **Own your own happiness**
> **Challenge your story**
> **Enjoy the journey not the destination**
> **Make relationships count**
> **Balance work with play**

What questions do I have?

NOTES

NOTES

Also available from Beyond Expectations Media

Built To Last

Making Difference Work

Chaos To Order

Through The Storm

Untying Fear Knots

Eye 2 Eye

GYMNASIUM
OF THE MIND

www.ingramcontent.com/pod-product-compliance
Lightning Source LLC
Chambersburg PA
CBHW041743040426
42444CB00001B/10